Report from the Judenplatz
Sue Boyle

Sue Boyle

REPORT FROM THE JUDENPLATZ

Time & Tide Publishing
BATH

COVER
Based on a photo design by
Dorielle Rimmer Halperin

ISBN-13:978-1482776294

timeandtidepublishing@gmail.com

REMEMBER
THAT THIS HAS BEEN

Meditate che questo è stato
Primo Levi

from
Alwyn Marriage
Managing Editor Oversteps Books

How can one speak of the unspeakable? Many poets and prose writers have attempted to write about the horrors of the Holocaust; but few have succeeded, as Sue Boyle has in this short book, in finding appropriate words that sing, that move and that linger long after the book is closed.

Sue approaches her difficult subject matter lightly and sensitively, gives no easy answers but leaves the reader feeling wiser and full of respect for those who suffered, rather than depressed. She also shows us that those fatal flaws in the human race, that wreaked such havoc in the twentieth century, are there right from the start in such ancient stories as Noah's Ark.

This series of beautiful poems can also form a dramatic reading, as Sue shows in Part 2 of the book.

Contents

Nine Lamentations

A Play for Witnesses

Notes

Foreword

The poems in *Report from the Judenplatz* are not directly about the 1939–1945 Nazi atrocities against the Jewish citizens of Europe. If we read attentively, the events in the concentration and extermination camps, and on the journeys to those camps, can be imagined by those of us who did not experience them, but the actual horror seems to me and many others a sacred space whose speaking should remain the prerogative of the victims and the survivors. We have a duty to know, to remember, to preserve and to honour their voices, but I am not sure that it is proper to create fictions of what we imagine their almost unspeakable experiences might have been.

Historical Europe, with its ubiquity of chapels, cathedrals and churches, seemed to declare itself a continent inspired by the values of Christianity. Its Christian citizens were instructed to love their neighbours as themselves, but every appropriated Jewish apartment, every emptied schoolroom chair, every silenced Jewish voice and every unasked question revealed the partiality of the Christian claim. The poems and the companion play for witnesses in *Report from the Judenplatz* mourn a colossal failure of compassion which did not begin in 1939 and did not end with the ending of that war.

This sequence of lamentations begins on Noah's Ark.

ark

You could not fault the construction. Gopher and cedar wood, every curve perfect to purpose, every joint tight as a tooth in its long jaw.

In later years people would compare the ark with a zeppelin, blind, monstrous and menacing, drifting across the apparent sky of the drowned world, turning its eyeless face away from those who were sinking in the dreadful sea.

In the morning the women scoured and scrubbed the deck, singing in unison. In the evening the men sang part songs and catches as they promenaded the chosen animals round and round the deck to get their exercise and fill of air.

In the wilderness beyond the boat the sea bobbed with the dead. Later, people would remember how the bodies drifted until they found havens, tangled in the branches of drowned trees, lodged in the rafts of debris, often with their mouths open as if still gasping for air, their eyes staring as if still greedy for the light.

In the early days, when many still lived, though doomed, those who could swim, or float, or cling to a floating thing would surround the wooden monolith, calling for rescue, banging on the pitiless sides, the animals too, swimming in its wake until exhaustion drowned them.

No face looked down. No one lowered a rope or a rescue raft. Some claim that the people on board even pushed creatures who did successfully scale the ark's clifflike sides back into the sea with poles and brooms saying it was their deity's will that only the chosen should be saved.

Some even say that the people on the boat were singing while their nearest neighbours drowned.

sunset at schönbrunn

At sunset they summon the keepers
and stroll to the Gloriette
with the lynx, the panther, the ocelot,
the family of brown bears.

From the terrace they see their city
to the south, the east, the west,
the domes, the spires, the opera houses,
greater than ever, glittering with life.

After me, says the child, Mozart,
his little silk breeches, rosebud buckled shoes,
the god will have nothing further to say to men.
There can be no music after me.
There will be no need for it.

After me, says Franz Joseph,
they will applaud the tanks,
ransack each other's houses
and brother make his brother
scrub the street with his poor bare hands.
There will be no pity in my Hofgarten.

the four good fortunes
of domenico

To be born in Padua
where every blue day
his mother could wheel his pram
among her friends in the handsome Prato:

E mio figlio, mio primogenito.
He will live long and be
a respected, unbroken man.

The Orto Botanico
those green hours and his father's call:

Come see this or this other thing
and learn its name as given by great Linnaeus.
Nothing of this will change
whatever black noise you hear beyond these walls.

His grandfather teaching him later
that what he knows is what makes a man,
not the race he comes from
nor his family name.

His uncle Reuben, the cantor
who lifts him up
above the crush and the roar
of the strange new voices:

Domenicino, hush.
We are good Italians.
They will not hurt us.

laura

my neighbour has a box of photographs
where she came from, whose daughter she was

the cameras caught the play of light on dark
but she knew every actor in the cast

the heroes, villains
troupe of walk-on parts

who strolled, who stumbled
muddled through their lines

where each was born, where everybody lived
what lasting good or passing harm they did

what stations saw them herded on to trains
what camp gates opened up to let them in

report from the judenplatz

Two idle waiters under an awning are talking quietly.

A man in a white suit with a black shoulder bag
and a dog, also white and black, a Pomeranian,
has taken the table adjacent to mine but just out of the sun
and the man is sending body signals
that he would very much welcome an encounter
with an attractive younger person of either sex.

Two upright old style bicycles
leaning as one on the painted wall of the Schneider house,
their pedals and handlebars interlocked like lovers' fingers –
their intricate shadows,
the meaningless abstract artistry of that.

There is also an armed guard
who conveys that waiting at the door
of a scarcely visited museum in the only dark corner
of an almost deserted square at her age is very dull.
She is blonde. She has a pistol, an automatic weapon
and a two-way radio.

On the low plinth of the Holocaust Memorial
a group of backpackers are sharing lunch.
Most of them have taken off their shoes.
One is oiling another's calf muscles.
They photograph each other. Girls redo their hair.

Auschwitz. Dachau. Theresienstadt – this generation
sits on the names of the places that swallowed us.
But the air in this place
has retained the print of no one's passing
nor do these stones cry out.

That is how it is today, *meine Liebe.*

That is how it is.

wintering in rome

Not even the exiled and unloved will stop today
in a city so estranged from itself in snow

to hear an old man with an accordion
who has set aside his usual repertoire

of Paris chansons, themes from *The Godfather*
and standards from the top Lloyd Webber shows.

From their cars and in their guard houses
the carabinieri protect the synagogue

while in the famous kosher restaurants
families and tourists take their lunch.

This is a place of a thousand absences –
Rachel, Eli, Judith, Joachim

children, rabbis, uncles, grandparents,
David, Ben Ezra, Sarah, Benjamin

who lived and worked
attended synagogue

and ate together in these restaurants
until their city turned its back on them.

The accordionist is playing their music now
their wedding song, their dance, their lullaby

their lullaby, their dance, their wedding song.

memorial plaque
in largo 16 ottobre
ghetto di roma

IL 16 OTTOBRE 1943
QUI EBBE INIZIO
LA SPIETATA CACCIA AGLI EBREI
E DUEMILANOVANTUNO CITTADINI ROMANI
VENNERO AVVIATI A FEROCE MORTE
NEI CAMPI DI STERMINIO NAZISTI
DOVE FURONE RAGGIUNTI
DA ALTRI SEIMILA ITALIANI
VITTIME DELL INFAME
ODIO DI RAZZA
I POCHI SCAMPATI ALLA STRAGE
I MOLTI SOLIDALI
INVOCANO DAGLI UOMINI
AMORE E PACE
INVOCANO DA DIO
PERDONO E SPERANZA

on 16 october 1943
here began
the pitiless hunting down of jews
and 2,091 roman citizens
were led to a ferocious death
in the nazi extermination camps
where they were joined
by another 6,000 italians
victims of infamous
race hatred
the few who escaped the massacre
and the many who now stand with them
cry out to men
for love and peace
and to god
for forgiveness and hope

A CURA COMITATO NAZIONALE
PER LE CELEBRAZIONI DEL VENTENNALE
DELLA RESISTENZA
25 OTTOBRE 1964

waterlilies at schönbrunn

i
Flowers, pale as wax,
a crowd of leaves,
beseeching light from the indifferent sun.
The anguish of distant bells, the trains,
curving their way across a continent
as the June heat builds.

ii
I will take my tools –
hammer, chisels, augur, whetstone, saw.
There is strength in my arm.
My eye is clear and true.
We shall need houses at this journey's end.
Life lies ahead and a builder is what I am,
a father said.

iii
There will be space for everything we need –
pianos, poems, songs, a violin
to stir the hearts of friends in shuttered rooms.
There is always music at a journey's end.
Life lies ahead and a singer is what I am,
a mother said.

iv
They will let me bring what makes me beautiful –
bracelets, ribbons, brushes for my hair.
A young man is waiting there to take my hand.
I shall be married at this journey's end.
Life lies ahead and my beauty is what I am,
a daughter said.

v
These are the gifts of my lovely shining life –
the new moon's arc, this star, this evening sky.
I am abundant with unfolding love.
Strong hands will hold me at this journey's end.
Life lies ahead and delight is what I am,
a baby said.

vi
Hamburg, Vienna, Salonica, Turin,
Leipzig, Bergen, Amsterdam, Berlin,
Padua, Paris, Avignon, Lublin,
Zagreb – the trains

vii
The empty trains returning.
The anguish of bells.
The pale of lotuses.

flown

There is no doubt that during the period of the migration and ultimate disappearance of the cultural and religious minorities in continental Europe the angels of Europe were also on the move.

The night air of many of the great cities was reported for a while to be thick with the brush of innumerable wings. At the same time by day subtle alterations were noticed as the angels vacated altar pieces, left curious gaps in fresco paintings, disappeared from psalteries, from illuminated manuscripts, from chapel ceilings and from their watch over Christian graves.

The process was not immediate. Angel figures first became translucent, paper thin or ghostly, depending on the medium in which they had been portrayed, as if the idea of the angel remained in place but the living creature had vacated the husk of its former self.

Some observers claimed to have seen the process of transformation and compared it to that of a dragonfly vacating its exuvia, the head and folded wings of each angel emerging into the world filmed in a fine white cocoon from which they had to struggle to break free.

People spoke of the unearthly colouring of these emerging creatures – how their bodies were not flesh-coloured, as our artists had portrayed them, but the non-colour of unembodied light, transparent, as though the whole creature were made of air, its wings simultaneously reflective of the light and near invisible.

It was clear at once that our artists had been utterly wrong to imagine that angels were like ourselves and therefore to have represented them in the traditional anthropomorphic way.

Angelic departures were noted in all the cities from which Europe's ethnic and religious minorities were transported on trains towards the resettlement areas in the east.

It was even said that rivers of angels flew alongside and above the windowless trains, causing a peculiar quietness in the air and silencing the birds in the areas through which they passed. In some areas, there are claims that from that time, the birds' dawn chorus was never heard again.

Since the resettlements of 1939–1945 there have been no reported sightings of angels in our continent and we must now, regrettably, assume that they are extinct.

styx

This river without reflection, which neither moves
Nor is affected by movement – is it water?
This medium we pass through – is it air?
Who will remember us?
Who will write our song?

Report from the Judenplatz

A Play for Witnesses

This play can be performed by any number of witnesses, with or without an audience. The witnesses can be positioned and directed in any way that suits the performance space. One idea for production is to seat the real audience on the illuminated stage with the witnesses positioned around the darkened auditorium. If enough performers are available, the stage can be filled with a seated 'audience' of actors, perhaps in period costume, who remain impassive through the performance while the witnesses speak from among the 'real' audience. The poster which forms the cover for this book, or appropriate black and white photographic images from European cities during the period of the 1939–1945 deportations can be displayed, or projected onto a screen above or behind the stage.

FIRST VOICE   ark

NEW VOICE   You could not fault the construction. Gopher and cedar wood, every curve perfect to purpose, every joint tight as a tooth in its long jaw.

NEW VOICE   In later years people would compare the ark with a zeppelin, monstrous and menacing, drifting across the apparent sky of the drowned world, turning its eyeless face away from those who were sinking in that dreadful sea.

NEW VOICE   In the morning the women scoured and scrubbed the deck, singing in unison. In the evening the men sang part songs and catches as they promenaded the chosen animals round and round the deck to get their exercise and fill of air.

NEW VOICE   In the wilderness beyond the boat, the sea bobbed with the dead. It would be remembered later how the bodies drifted until they found havens, tangled in the branches of drowned trees, lodged in the rafts of debris, often with their mouths open as if still gasping for air, their eyes staring as if still greedy for the light.

NEW VOICE   In the early days, when many still lived, though doomed, those who could swim, or float, or cling to a floating thing would surround the wooden monolith, calling for rescue, banging on the pitiless sides, the animals too, swimming in its wake until exhaustion drowned them.

NEW VOICE   No face looked down. No one lowered a rope or a rescue raft. Some claim that the people on board even pushed creatures who did successfully scale the ark's clifflike sides back into the sea with poles and brooms saying it was their deity's will that only the chosen should be saved.

NEW VOICE   Some even say that the people on the boat were
singing while their nearest neighbours drowned.

NEW VOICE   ## sunset at schönbrunn

NEW VOICE   At sunset they summon the keepers
and stroll to the Gloriette
with the lynx, the panther, the ocelot,
the family of brown bears.

NEW VOICE   From the terrace they see their city
to the south, the east, the west,
the domes, the spires, the opera houses,
greater than ever, glittering with life.

NEW VOICE   After me, says the child, Mozart,
his little silk breeches, rosebud buckled shoes,
the god has nothing further to say to men.
There will be no music after me.
There will be no need for it.

NEW VOICE   After me, says Franz Joseph,
they will applaud the foreign tanks,
ransack each other's houses
and brother make his brother
scrub the street with his poor bare hands.
There will be no pity in my Hofgarten.

NEW VOICE   ## the four good fortunes of domenico

NEW VOICE   To be born in Padua
where every blue day
his mother could wheel his pram
among her friends in the handsome Prato:

NEW VOICE   *E mio figlio, mio primogenito.*
He will live long and be
a respected, unbroken man.

NEW VOICE   The Orto Botanico
             those green hours and his father's call:

NEW VOICE   *Come see this or this other thing*
             and learn its name as given by great Linnaeus.
             Nothing of this will change
             whatever black noise you hear beyond these walls.

NEW VOICE   His grandfather teaching him later
             that what he knows is what makes a man,
             not the race he comes from
             nor his family name.

NEW VOICE   His uncle Reuben, the cantor
             who lifts him up
             above the crush and the roar
             of the strange new voices:

NEW VOICE   *Domenicino, hush.*
             We are good Italians
             They will not hurt us.

NEW VOICE   laura

NEW VOICE   my neighbour has a box of photographs
             where she came from, whose daughter she was

NEW VOICE   the cameras caught the play of light on dark
             but she knew every actor in the cast

NEW VOICE   the heroes, villains, troupe of walk-on parts
             who strolled, who stumbled
             muddled through their lines

NEW VOICE   where each was born, where everybody lived
             what lasting good or passing harm they did

NEW VOICE   what stations saw them herded on to trains
             what camp gates opened up to let them in

NEW VOICE a report from the judenplatz

NEW VOICE Two idle waiters under an awning
are talking quietly.

NEW VOICE A man in a white suit with a black shoulder bag
and a dog, also white and black, a Pomeranian,
has taken the table adjacent to mine
but just out of the sun
and the man is sending body signals
that he would very much welcome an encounter
with an attractive younger person of either sex.

NEW VOICE Two upright old style bicycles leaning as one
on the painted wall of the Schneider house,
their pedals and handlebars interlocked
like lovers' fingers, their intricate shadows,
the meaningless abstract artistry of that.

NEW VOICE There is also an armed guard
who conveys that waiting at the door
of a scarcely visited museum
in the only dark corner
of an almost deserted square
at her age is very dull.
She is blonde. She has a pistol,
an automatic weapon
and a two-way radio.

NEW VOICE On the low plinth of the Holocaust Memorial
a group of backpackers are sharing lunch.
Most of them have taken off their shoes.
One is oiling another's calf muscles.
They photograph each other. Girls redo their hair.
Auschwitz. Dachau. Theresienstadt –
this generation
sits on the names of the places that swallowed us.

NEW VOICE But the air in this place has retained
the print of no one's passing

nor do these stones cry out.

NEW VOICE   That is how it is today, *meine Liebe.*
     That is how it is.

NEW VOICE   wintering in rome

NEW VOICE   Not even the exiled and unloved will stop today
     in a city so estranged from itself in snow
     to hear an old man with an accordion
     who has set aside his usual repertoire
     of Paris chansons, themes from *The Godfather*
     and standards from the top Lloyd Webber shows.

NEW VOICE   From their cars and in their guard houses
     the carabinieri protect the synagogue
     while in the famous kosher restaurants
     families and tourists take their lunch.

NEW VOICE   This is a place of a thousand absences –
     Rachel, Eli, Judith, Joachim,
     children, rabbis, uncles, grandparents,
     David, Ben Ezra, Sarah, Benjamin

NEW VOICE   who lived and worked
     attended synagogue
     and ate together in these restaurants
     until their city turned its back on them.

NEW VOICE   The accordionist is playing their music now
     their wedding song, their dance, their lullaby

NEW VOICE   Their lullaby, their dance, their wedding song.

NEW VOICE   waterlilies at schönbrunn

NEW VOICE   Flowers, pale as wax,
     a crowd of leaves,
     beseeching light from the indifferent sun,
     the anguish of bells, the trains

curving their way across a continent
as the June heat builds.

NEW VOICE   I will take my tools –
hammer, chisels, augur, whetstone, saw.
There is strength in my arm.
My eye is clear and true.
We shall need houses at this journey's end:
life lies ahead and a builder is what I am,
a father said.

NEW VOICE   There will be room for everything we need –
pianos, poems, songs, a violin
to stir the hearts of friends in shuttered rooms.
There is always music at a journey's end:
life lies ahead and a singer is what I am,
a mother said.

NEW VOICE   They will let me bring what makes me beautiful –
bracelets, ribbons, brushes for my hair.
A young man is waiting there to take my hand.
I shall be married at this journey's end:
life lies ahead and my beauty is what I am,
a daughter said.

NEW VOICE   These are the gifts of my lovely shining life –
the new moon's arc, this star, this evening sky.
I am abundant with unfolding love.
Strong hands will hold me at this journey's end:
a baby said.

NEW VOICE   Hamburg, Vienna, Salonica, Turin,
Leipzig, Bergen, Amsterdam, Berlin,
Padua, Paris, Avignon, Lublin,
Zagreb – the trains.

NEW VOICE   The empty trains returning.

NEW VOICE   The anguish of bells.

NEW VOICE   The pale of lotuses.

NEW VOICE   flown

NEW VOICE   There is no doubt that during the period of the migration and ultimate disappearance of the cultural and religious minorities in continental Europe, the angels of Europe were also on the move.

NEW VOICE   The night air of many of the great cities was reported for a while to be thick with the brush of innumerable wings and at the same time by day subtle alterations were noticed as the angels vacated altar pieces, left curious gaps in fresco paintings, disappeared from psalteries, from illuminated manuscripts, from chapel ceilings and from their watch over Christian graves.

NEW VOICE   The process was not immediate. Angel figures first became translucent, paper thin or ghostly, depending on the medium in which they had been portrayed, as if the idea of the angel remained in place but the living creature had vacated the husk of its former self.

NEW VOICE   Some observers claimed to have seen the process of transformation and compared it to that of a dragonfly vacating its exuvia, the head and folded wings of each angel emerging into the world filmed in a fine white cocoon from which they had to struggle to break free.

NEW VOICE   People spoke of the unearthly colouring of these emerging creatures – how their bodies were not flesh-coloured, as our artists had portrayed them, but the non-colour of unembodied light, transparent, as though the whole creature were made of air, its wings simultaneously reflective of the light and near invisible.

NEW VOICE   It was clear at once that our artists had been utterly wrong to imagine that angels were like ourselves and therefore to have represented them in the traditional anthropomorphic way.

NEW VOICE   Angelic departures were noted in all the cities from which Europe's ethnic and religious minorities were transported on trains towards the resettlement areas in the east.

NEW VOICE   It was even said that rivers of angels flew alongside and above the windowless trains, causing a peculiar quietness in the air and silencing the birds in the areas through which they passed. In some areas, there are claims that from that time, the birds' dawn chorus was never heard again.

NEW VOICE   Since the resettlements of 1939–1945 there have been no reported sightings of angels in our continent and we must now, regrettably, assume that they are extinct.

NEW VOICE   styx

NEW VOICE   This river without reflection,
which neither moves nor is affected by movement –
is it water?

NEW VOICE   This medium we pass through – is it air?

NEW VOICE   Who will remember us?

LAST VOICE   Who will write our song?

Notes

These notes have been compiled from a variety of sources. I am particularly indebted to many online witnesses, researchers and historians for their accounts of the Kindertransports, of what happened to the Jews in Vienna and of the deportations from Padua and from the Rome ghetto in 1943.

laura

The persecution of German Jews began after the Nazi party came to power in January 1933. World Jewish Relief, then called 'The Central British Fund for German Jewry', was established a few months later to support the urgent needs of the Jews of Germany and Austria. A stream of Jewish refugees began to leave Germany, a process that accelerated when the German Government enacted the Nuremberg Laws in September 1935. Following the devastation of Kristallnacht in Germany and Austria on 9 November 1938, World Jewish Relief embarked on a rescue operation which saved the lives of thousands of children. Within three weeks 200 Jewish children were assembled in Germany to travel by train via the Hook of Holland to Harwich in the UK. The Kindertransport had begun. In the next nine months over 10,000 unaccompanied, mainly Jewish, children travelled to the UK on the Kindertransports. Most of them journeyed on from Harwich to Liverpool Street Station in London where they met their volunteer foster parents for the first time. On the Liverpool Street station concourse there is now a commemorative bronze by Israeli sculptor Frank Meisler who arrived from Danzig on one of the Kindertransports in 1939.

the four good fortunes of domenico

Following Italy's capitulation on 8 September 1943, and the subsequent invasion by the German Wehrmacht, a large area of Northern Italy officially became the Italian Social Republic, a fascist puppet state under German occupation. Not long after the invasion, the Germans set up an internment camp for Italian prisoners of war in a rice mill in Trieste. At the end of October 1943 this was transformed into a police detention camp. The camp known as Risiera di San Sabba is now a museum of commemoration for victims of the occupation and the Holocaust. Thousands of prisoners, among them Jews from Fiume, Trieste and Padua, were deported to concentration or death camps from San Sabba. The deportations of the Jews of Padua started on 3 December 1943. Of those deported from Padua to Auschwitz in 1944, only three returned. On 29 April 1945 the camp at San Sabba was dissolved. In an attempt to erase evidence of the murders which took place there, the camp personnel blew up the crematorium before taking flight. The total number of victims of the Nazi extermination in Italy is estimated at 8,529, or 26·24 per cent of the entire Jewish population living in Italy just before the German occupation.

wintering in rome

The roundup of Roman Jews began on 16 October 1943. The Germans surrounded the Ghetto on Shabbat and went door-to-door in the early morning waking up the Jews on their list of addresses. They were given twenty minutes to assemble their possessions and assemble outside in the rain. 1,000 Jews – 900 of whom were women and children – were taken to the Military College of Rome only a few blocks from St Peter's Basilica. Owen Chadwick estimates the number of deportees to Auschwitz at 1,007 and the number of survivors at 15. Susan Zuccotti's research in *Under His Very Windows: The Vatican and the Holocaust in Italy* demonstrates that the Pope did not, as is sometimes claimed, give orders to the various Roman Catholic institutions of Rome to open their doors to the Jews. In October 2000 a stone plaque was unveiled at the Tiburtina railway station, the site of the deportations, to honour the memory of the Jews deported from the city on 16 October 1943. The plaque appeared to observers no longer to have a place when the renovated station was officially opened on 28 November 2011 in the presence of the President of the Italian Republic, Giorgio Napolitano.

'MEDITATE CHE QUESTO
È STATO'
Primo Levi

IL 16 OTTOBRE 1943
PIÙ DI MILLE EBREI ROMANI,
INTERE FAMIGLIE, UOMINI DONNE E BAMBINI,
VENNERO STRAPPATI ALLE LORO CASE,
COLPEVOLI SOLO DI ESISTERE.
DA QUESTA STAZIONE RACCHIUSI IN CARRI
PIOMBATI
IL 18 OTTOBRE
VENNERO DAI NAZISTI DEPORTATI
NEI CAMPI DI STERMINIO.
SEDICI UOMINI E SOLO UNA DONNA
FECERO RITORNO.
LA LORO MEMORIA
E QUELLA DI TUTTI I DEPORTATI ROMANI,
EBREI, POLITICI, MILITARI, LAVORATORI,
SIA MONITO PERENNE
PERCHÈ OVUNQUE SIMILI TRAGEDIE
NON DEBANNO ESSERE RIVISSUTE.
MAI PIÙ

COMUNE DI ROMA
ASSOCIAZIONE NAZIONALE EX DEPORTATI
NEI CAMPI NAZISTI
COMUNITÀ EBRAICA DI ROMA
16 OTTOBRE 2000

'REMEMBER THAT THIS HAS BEEN'

Primo Levi

ON 16 OCTOBER 1943
MORE THAN ONE THOUSAND ROMAN JEWS,
ENTIRE FAMILIES, MEN, WOMEN AND CHILDREN,
GUILTY ONLY OF EXISTING,
WERE SEIZED FROM THEIR HOMES.
AT THIS STATION THEY WERE SEALED INTO TRUCKS.
ON 18 OCTOBER
THEY WERE DEPORTED BY THE NAZIS
TO EXTERMINATION CAMPS.
SIXTEEN MEN AND ONLY ONE WOMAN
RETURNED.
LET THEIR MEMORY
AND THE MEMORY OF ALL THOSE DEPORTED FROM ROME –
JEWS, POLITICIANS, SERVICEMEN, WORKERS –
BE A PERPETUAL WARNING
SO THAT NOWHERE IN THE WORLD
WILL SUCH A TRAGEDY EVER OCCUR AGAIN.
NEVER AGAIN.

COMUNE DI ROMA
ASSOCIAZIONE NAZIONALE EX DEPORTATI
NEI CAMPI NAZISTI
COMUNITÀ EBRAICA DI ROMA
16 OTTOBRE 2000

waterlilies at schönbrunn

In January 1938 there were approximately 190,000 Jews living in Austria. One third of these were no longer alive in May 1945. The real terror for most of the Jewish population began on 12 March 1938 when the German army marched into and annexed the First Republic of Austria. A plebiscite in Austria on 10 April 1938 resulted in over 99 percent of the eligible population – Jews and other 'unwanted' citizens were not allowed to vote – voting in favour of the German annexation. Within months, all Jews in Austria were ordered to move to Vienna, and then eventually to the 2nd district, Leopoldstadt, where there had once been a Jewish ghetto. SS Second Lieutenant Adolf Eichmann (like Adolf Hitler a native of Austria) soon established a 'model' in Austria for solving 'the Jewish problem'. His plan was to evict the Jews and keep as much of their assets as possible. He set up a Central Office of Jewish Emigration in the 'Aryanized' Rothschild palace in Prinz-Eugen-Strasse, across from the Belvedere. By December 1940 there were still about 50,000 to 60,000 Jews living in Vienna. The first systematic deportations to the Łódź Ghetto began on 15 October 1941. Deportations to Minsk, Riga and Terezín (Theresienstadt) followed. The first deportation directly to Auschwitz took place on 17 July 1942. The deportations continued into 1945. By the end of the war there were approximately 5,000 Jews left in Austria.

sunset at schönbrunn
report from the judenplatz

Four years after I wrote these two poems from Vienna, I read an article which had first appeared in the *Washington Post* on 24 June 1990. The author, Michael Z. Wise, is now Vice President of New Vessel Press in New York and has very kindly given me permission to use this short digest of his much longer piece. He is writing about Austrian artist Alfred Hrdlicka's bronze, sited between the Opera House and the Albertina, which depicts an elderly Viennese Jew forced to kneel and scrub the streets after Austria was annexed by Germany in 1938. Such public degradation and cruelty were widespread following the annexation and presaged the deportation of more than 60,000 Austrian Jews to the gas chambers. In 1990

Jews and Viennese city officials alike were disturbed that the sculpture was failing to achieve the anticipated impact on visitors. From time to time a wreath or solitary rose had been seen beside the bronze figure, but its patina also bore the stains of countless dogs who had defiled it as their owners stood by. Worse still, foreign tourists, weary from sightseeing and apparently oblivious to the sculpture's significance, were treating the kneeling figure as if it were a park bench. Viennese director Robert Polak documented this in a short film distributed to city schools as part of the Holocaust education programme. The film included footage of tourists stepping on to the sculpture, sipping drinks as they sat on top of it and posing for snapshots while they lounged across its surface. 'I saw this happening and wanted to make a film of observation,' said Polak. 'I did not lie in wait to find this. I simply went there five times with a video camera.'

cover design

The cover design for this book is by Dorielle Rimmer Halperin, a graduate of the Bezalel Academy of Arts and Design in Jerusalem. The design won first prize in Yad Vashem's 2012 competition for an official poster for Holocaust Martyrs' and Heroes' Remembrance Day and has been very kindly made available by the Yad Vashem Museum in Jerusalem.

the yad vashem museum

The Yad Vashem Museum, established in 1953 through the Yad Vashem Law passed by the Knesset, Israel's parliament, is Israel's official memorial to the Jewish victims of the Holocaust. The name Yad Vashem is taken from a verse in the Book of Isaiah: 'Even unto them will I give in mine house and within my walls a place and a name (yad vashem) better than of sons and of daughters: I will give them an everlasting name that shall not be cut off' (Isaiah 56:5). Yad Vashem seeks to preserve the memory and names of the six million Jews murdered during the Holocaust and of the numerous Jewish communities destroyed during that time. It holds ceremonies of remembrance and commemoration; supports Holocaust research projects; develops and coordinates symposia, workshops and international conferences; and publishes research, memoirs, documents, albums and diaries related to the Holocaust. The museum combines the personal stories of 90 Holocaust victims and survivors and presents approximately 2,500 personal items including artwork and letters donated by survivors and others. The old historical displays revolving around anti-semitism and the rise of Nazism have been replaced by exhibits that focus on the personal stories of Jews killed in the Holocaust. According to Avner Shalev, the museum's curator and chairman, a visit to the new museum revolves around 'looking into the eyes of the individuals. There weren't six million victims, there were six million individual murders.' The Secretary-General of the United Nations, Kofi Annan, commented at the opening, 'The number of Holocaust survivors who are still with us is dwindling fast. Our children are growing up just as rapidly. They are beginning to ask their first questions about injustice. What will we tell them? Will we say, That's just the way the world is? Or will we say instead, We are trying to change things – to find a better way?'

Acknowledgements

I am very grateful to the editors of *Acumen*, *Poetry Salzburg* and *The Rialto* in which four of these poems first appeared and to Smith/ Doorstop for publishing 'Laura' and 'The Four Good Fortunes of Domenico' in *Too Late for the Love Hotel* which was one of the prize-winners in *The North*'s 2010 pamphlet competition judged by the Poet Laureate Andrew Motion.

'Waterlilies at Schönbrunn' was chosen, by Matt Holland, organiser of Holocaust Memorial Day events in Swindon on 27th January 2014, as the keynote poem for the day. It was read at both the formal ceremony at the town's Cenotaph and the subsequent gathering at the Friends Meeting House.

Report from the Judenplatz was performed for the first time as a play for witnesses on Friday 23 October 2014 at the Torbay Festival of Poetry under the direction of John Miles, winner of South Devon Drama Federation's 'Best Production Award' in 2012. The actors in this first performance were Brenda Hutchings, John Miles, Suzy Miles, William Oxley, David Perman, Rik Wilkinson and Pamela Williams.

On Tuesday 27 January 2015, I was invited to read three poems from *Report from the Judenplatz* at 'A Moment of Reflection', the Holocaust Memorial Day ceremony in Bath Guildhall, led by the Chairman of Bath and North East Somerset Council, Councillor Martin Veal. On the same day, in Swindon, Matt Holland again chose 'Waterlilies at Schönbrunn' for his reading at the Cenotaph.

I dedicated my reading at the Guildhall to Yohan Cohen, Yoav Hattab, Philippe Braham and François-Michel Saada, murdered in Porte de Vincennes, Paris on Friday 9 January 2015.

from Matt Holland
Director Swindon Festival of Literature & Lower Shaw Farm

What is it about Sue Boyle's *Report from the Judenplatz* that reads so well, that informs so clearly, and that moves me so?

While being entirely serious and writing with insight and respect, Sue has managed to avoid undue solemnity or long-windedness, both of which are tendencies that seduce many writers and speakers when dealing with this subject. It is so easy to suppose that big, long, laboured, Latinate words are needed to deal with the gravity of genocide. Sue has faith in plain words, key points, and brevity. It's as if she knows that detail is important and stories too but that, for the reader and hearer to be informed, engaged, and moved by her words, she must trust the reader's imagination and their own experiences.

The four central stanzas of 'Waterlilies at Schönbrunn' tell of journeys, both actual and figurative, that are universal and timeless. I find them deeply meaningful and moving.

And the shape of the book as a whole, its three key sections, makes this unusually powerful slim volume both accessible and beautiful. That's what I find anyway. A Play for Witnesses can be done by anyone, any voices. The words will carry you along. And the Notes section is neat, informative, and to the points that matter.

When a copy of *Report from the Judenplatz* landed on the mat, my day changed, my coffee break was extended, and I'd found words that were timely and to the point. Here was writing that helped me acknowledge dreadful facts, know significant stories, tackle tricky thoughts, and allow for key feelings; and showed me how to share them all with others. Thank you Sue.

Matt Holland, Director
Swindon Festival of Literature & Lower Shaw Farm

Dorielle Rimmer Halperin

I am very grateful to the Yad Vashem Museum in Jerusalem for permission to use Dorielle Rimmer Halperin's winning poster from the museum's 2012 competition as the cover design for this book, and to writer and publisher Michael Z. Wise for permission to use material from his 1990 *Washington Post* article on the Albert Hrdlicka bronze outside the Albertina in Vienna.

Dorielle Rimmer Halperin dedicated the poster to her grandparents who survived the Holocaust, as well as to their family members who did not. 'My design shows that the shadow of the family lying on the road is the shadow of the family who perished and will always be there with the survivors. But this is also the shadow of their new family of survivors, which is there to remember, to preserve them and their heroism. When I look at my grandparents, both Holocaust survivors, in their shadow I see my shadow as well. The lack of light in their lives is always there and will always be a part of me and my family, something we will pass on to future generations.'

Michael Z. Wise

Michael Z. Wise writes about architecture, culture and foreign affairs. His writing has appeared in many publications including *The Atlantic Monthly*, *Foreign Policy*, the *New York Times*, the *Los Angeles Times*, *The New Republic* and *ARTnews*. He has worked as a foreign correspondent in Vienna, Prague and London, reporting for Reuters and the *Washington Post*. Now an independent journalist based in New York, Michael Z. Wise is co-founder of New Vessel Press, a new ebook publishing company specialising in translations of foreign literature and literary non-fiction into English.

Sue Boyle

L'amore. La morte. How close they are.
The confusion of signs. The fiction of surfaces.

Sue Boyle's *Too Late for the Love Hotel* was a prizewinner in *The North*'s 2010 pamphlet competition judged by the Poet Laureate Sir Andrew Motion who said that the collection stood out because of 'the attention the poems pay to their subjects' and 'the range and strangeness of its interests.' A Londoner by family and background, she has lived in ten English counties and worked variously as an academic, a teacher, social worker, antiquarian print dealer, market trader in bric-a-brac and as a maker of specialist hand-finished picture frames. For the past six years she has organised the Bath Poetry Cafe and the associated Cafe Writing Days.

'Sue Boyle's is the voice of a true original: her work has a wit and inventiveness all too rare in poetry today.' (Rosie Bailey)

Time & Tide Publishing
BATH

38789082R00032

Made in the USA
Charleston, SC
19 February 2015